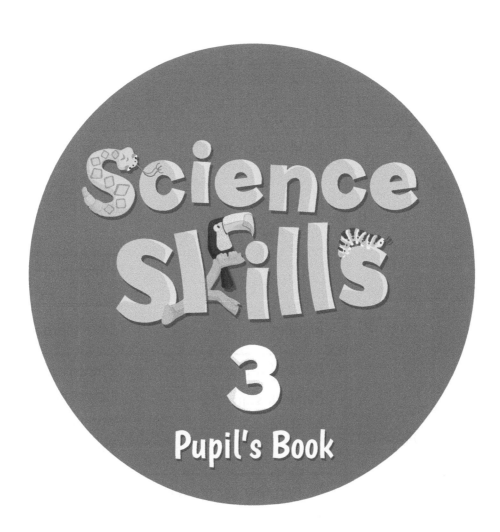

# Science Skills

## 3

### Pupil's Book

by

Margaret Stark

CAMBRIDGE
UNIVERSITY PRESS

# SCIENCE SKILLS 3

## Contents

- Nervous system
- Locomotor system
- Sense of hearing
- Sense of sight
- Senses of smell and taste
- Sense of touch

- Food groups and nutrients
- Digestive system
- Circulatory system
- Respiratory system
- Excretory system
- Healthy habits

- Mammals
- Birds
- Reptiles
- Amphibians
- Fish
- Invertebrates

- Parts of a plant
- Plant classification by stem
- Plant reproduction: flowering plants and non-flowering plants
- Plant nutrition

- Matter: changes of state
- Types of energy: light, thermal, sound, kinetic and electrical
- Materials: conductors and insulators
- Mixtures

- Simple machines: inclined plane, screw, pulley, wheel and axle, lever and wedge
- Inventions: steam engine and telegraph

| Projects and experiments | Documentaries |
|---|---|
| • Make a mural about a season and the five senses<br>• Build a pinhole camera | • Helping the senses |
| • Write a rap about nutrition<br>• Build a model of the respiratory system | • Say no to fast food |
| • Give a presentation about animals<br>• Find out why animals use camouflage | • The animal kingdom |
| • Make a field journal about plants<br>• Germinate a seed | • The plant kingdom |
| • Create signs to remind people to save water and energy<br>• Observe the effect of thermal energy on liquids | • Energy and matter |
| • Design a complex machine<br>• Communicate using Morse code | • Incredible inventions |

**More hands on**  Page 90

# WELCOME TO CAMBRIDGE SCIENCE SKILLS

Welcome to the amazing world of natural science. In this book, you will:

make a mural

help save the planet

invent a machine

go on safari

investigate plants

perform a rap

**You will also find out:**

- how fast your heart beats
- which vertebrates have two lives
- how to tell how old a tree is
- how to find gold
- how to make a car.

# 1

# WHY DO BABIES HAVE MORE BONES THAN ADULTS?

## Look and see ...

Name the senses in the photos.

Can you name any bones on the skeleton?

S🎵ng
Five senses

What do joints do?

What do muscles do?

D▶CUMENTARY
Helping the senses

# investigate

In this unit, you will make a mural about a season and the five senses.
To do this, you will:

- choose a season and think about what it reminds you of.
- learn about the five senses.
- think about how your senses help you enjoy the seasons.

# HOW DOES YOUR BRAIN WORK?

Body systems are made up of organs[1]. The **brain** is the organ which controls everything we do. It is the control centre of the **nervous system**.

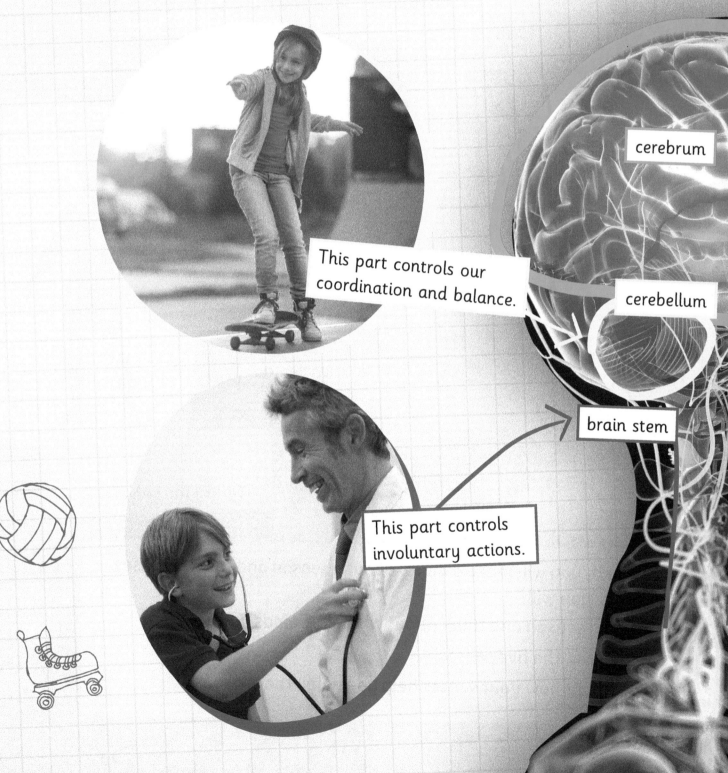

This part controls our coordination and balance.

This part controls involuntary actions.

cerebrum

cerebellum

brain stem

Do you remember what the sense organs are?

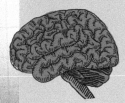

Our sense organs send information to our brain. This information travels to our brain through the **nerves**.

The brain then sends information back, through the nerves, to different parts of the body.

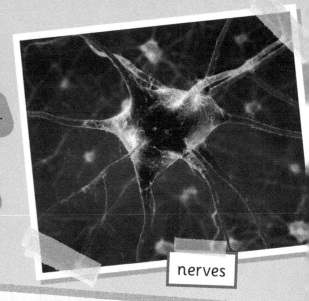

nerves

This part controls voluntary actions.

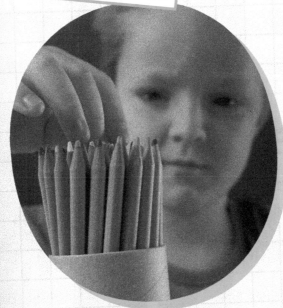

Which part of the brain helps us to dance?

## Investigate    STAGE 1

- Choose one of the four seasons.
- Quickly write down five things it reminds you of.
- Compare your list with a partner.

I've chosen … It reminds me of …

[1] **organ:** a part of the body that does an important job in a body system

9

# WHY DO YOU HAVE A SKELETON?

By the end of this lesson, you will know what the parts of the locomotor system are.

The **locomotor system** allows us to move. It has three main parts.

**Joints** are where our bones connect to each other.

**Muscles** are soft and elastic. They help us move.

Can you find the *skull*, *ribs* and *spinal column* in the skeleton?

**Bones** are hard and rigid. They form our **skeleton**, which gives our body shape.

Adults have 206 bones in their body. Babies have about 300 bones when they are born. Some of these bones later join together and become one.

Muscles work by **contracting** and **expanding**. Some muscles are *voluntary* — they only work when our brain tells them to. Other muscles are *involuntary* and they work automatically — like the heart.

Find the skeleton hidden in the unit.

# WHY DO YOU HAVE EARWAX?

By the end of this lesson, you will know how we can look after our hearing.

Our senses allow us to **interact** with the world around us. Our **sense of hearing** allows us to distinguish between different sounds.

1 Sound waves enter the **outer ear**.

2 They continue to the **middle ear** and make the **eardrum** vibrate.

3 These vibrations make the liquid in the **inner ear** move.

4 This movement sends information to the **brain**.

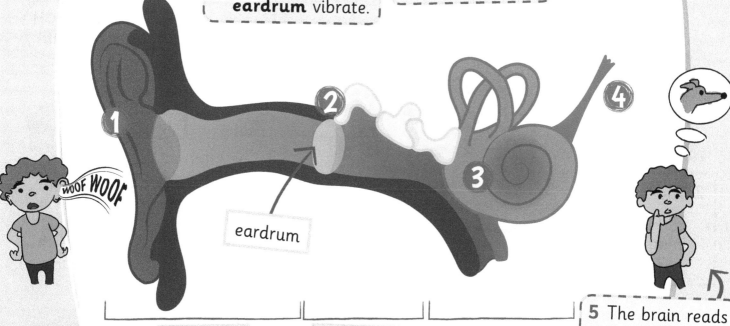

eardrum

outer ear    middle ear    inner ear

5 The brain reads the information and tells us what we are listening to.

🎧 Listen. What sounds can you hear?

## Investigate    STAGE 2

- What sounds can you hear during your season?
- Did you mention any of these sounds in Stage 1?
- Print out pictures of the things you can hear and write sentences about them.

### Look after your ears.

Our ears produce a sticky substance called earwax. Earwax protects our ears from dirt and infection.

## WHICH PART OF YOUR EYE IS SIMILAR TO A CAT'S WHISKERS?

Our **sense of sight** allows us to perceive shapes, size, movement, distance and colour.

**4** The brain reads the signal and tells us what we are seeing.

**1** Light reflects off an object and enters the eye.

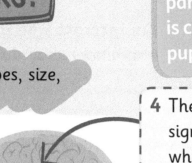

LUNCH TIME!

**3** The information is sent to the **brain**.

**2** The light forms an upside-down image on the **retina**.

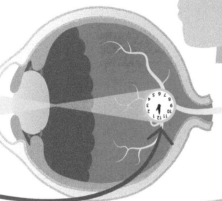

eyelashes

eyebrow

eyelid

Eyelashes protect the eye from dust and sweat. Also, if something is too close to your eye, your eyelashes sense it and warn you … in the same way that a cat's whiskers do.

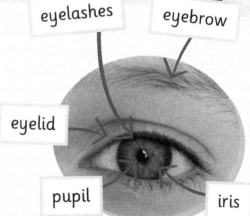

pupil

iris

Find out how to look after your eyes.

## Investigate STAGE 3

There are beautiful / amazing / interesting …

- **Think about what you can see during your season.**
- **Draw and colour pictures of the things you can see.**
- **Compare your pictures with a partner using different adjectives.**

## UPSIDE-DOWN IMAGES

## Hands on...

**Before you start**
The image that forms on the back of the eye (the retina) is upside-down.

**Materials**
cardboard tube, wax paper, tape, black card, elastic bands, aluminium foil, drawing pin

**Method**

1 Cover one end of the cardboard tube with wax paper and secure it with tape.

2 Cut out a piece of black card, the same length as the tube. Cover half of the tube with the card and secure it with an elastic band.

3 Cover the end of the black card with alumnium foil.

4 Make a small hole in the aluminium foil with the pin.

5 Point the camera at an object. You can zoom in or out by moving the black card.

**Conclusions**
What happened to the object when you looked at it through the camera?

Which part of the pinhole camera functions as the pupil?

Which part of the pinhole camera functions as the retina?

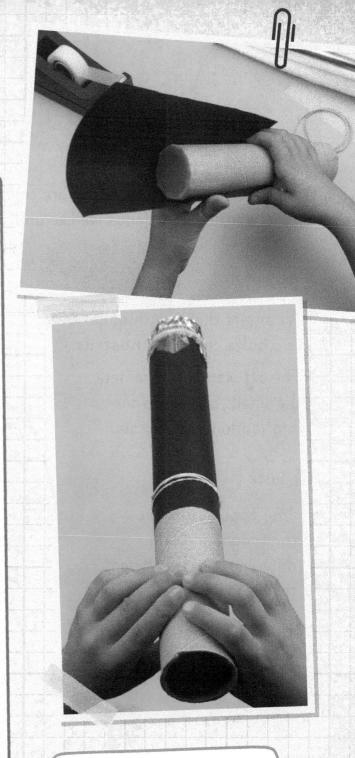

The ... functions as the ...

The camera formed an ... image.

Why should you not touch the pupil of your eye?

# HOW DO YOU KNOW IF POPCORN IS SWEET OR SALTY?

By the end of this lesson, you will know how information about different smells and tastes pass to the brain.

Our senses of **smell** and **taste** are connected. These senses help us decide which foods we like and which we do not like.

## Smell

1 Air enters the nose through two holes called the **nostrils**.

2 The **olfactory nerve** detects the smells and sends the information to the brain.

## Taste

1 Tiny **taste buds** on the tongue identify different tastes. Different tastes can be identified anywhere on the tongue.

2 This information is sent to the brain via the **nerves**.

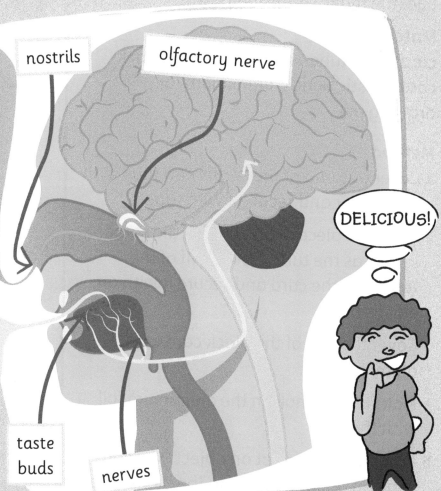

nostrils

olfactory nerve

DELICIOUS!

taste buds

nerves

# Investigate    STAGE 4

- **What can you smell and taste during your season?**
- **Do you eat any typical foods at this time of the year?**
- **Make a menu for your season with pictures.**

There are four main tastes: sweet, salty, bitter and sour.

Find out how to look after your nose and mouth.

How do the foods on pages 6 and 7 taste?

## HOW DOES YOUR SKIN STOP YOU GETTING BURNT?

By the end of this lesson, you will know which nerves send information about how things feel to the brain.

How do we know that a tree feels rough, but a jumper feels soft? Our body is covered in **skin** and our skin is the organ of **touch**.

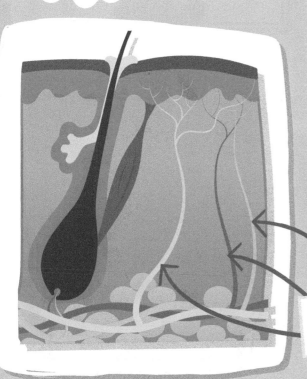

Our skin tells us if something is rough, smooth, hard or soft. **Sensory nerves** below the skin send information to the brain when we touch something. If something is too hot, our skin will tell us!

sensory nerves

Rain!

### How do these things feel?

## Investigate STAGE 5

- What things can you touch during your season?
- Search for pictures of them on the internet.
- Label the pictures with adjectives to describe how they feel.

Find out how to look after your skin.

15

**1** 🎧 **Listen and match the names with the numbers in your notebook. There is one example.**

Dan  Matt  Tom  Sally  Jane  Daisy *e*  Anna

**2** **Choose the correct verb in the past tense.**
a The lemons ..... sour. (*tasted* / *taste*)
b The bark of a tree ..... rough. (*feel* / *felt*)
c We ..... a beautiful dog. (*saw* / *seed*)
d The pizzas ..... delicious. (*smelt* / *smeled*)
e My singing ..... horrible! (*sounded* / *sound*)

**1** Write the parts of the brain (1–3) in your notebook. Match them to what they control (a–c).

   a  Involuntary actions

   b  Balance and coordination

   c  Voluntary actions

**2** Which picture is the odd one out? Explain why.

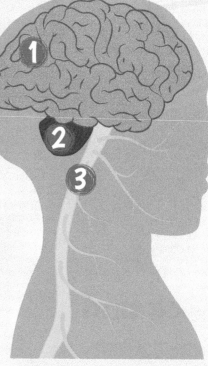

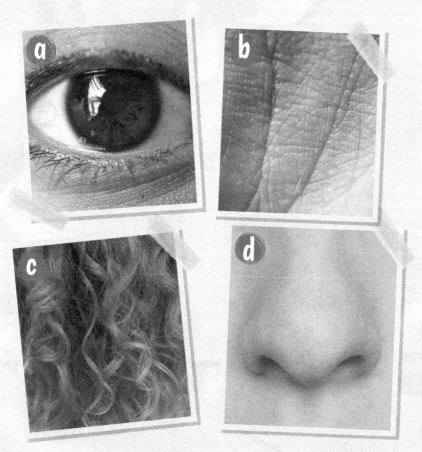

My favourite season is autumn. The leaves on the trees change colour and we can see …

# Investigate     FINALE

- Make a mural about your season and the senses. Include the pictures and information you found.

- Practise describing your mural with a partner.

- Display your work for everyone to see and enjoy.

## Assessment link

Go to page 78 for more activities.

# 2

# WHAT HAPPENS TO FOOD INSIDE YOUR BODY?

Can you name the food groups in these pictures?

**Look and see...**

How often do you eat unhealthy food?

What things are important to keep us healthy?

**S☺ng**
A journey inside the human body

**D⏵CUMENTARY**
Say no to fast food

# Investigate

In this unit, you will write a rap about nutrition and the body systems.
To do this, you will:

- identify the main organs in each body system and learn what they do.

- understand how the body systems work together to perform the process of nutrition.

- perform your rap for your classmates.

# HOW CAN YOU STAY STRONG?

If pizza is your favourite food, why can you not eat it every day? You need to eat a balanced[1] mixture of foods to stay healthy. This is because different **food groups** contain different things that your body needs. These things are called **nutrients**.

## Carbohydrates and fibre

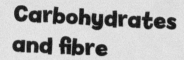

Grains, cereals and potatoes contain **carbohydrates**. Carbohydrates give us energy. They also contain **fibre** which is good for our digestive system.

What should you always do before eating?

## Proteins and iron

Meat, fish, nuts and beans contain a lot of **proteins** and **iron**. They make our muscles strong and help us grow.

20

## Dairy

Dairy products, such as milk and cheese, contain a lot of **calcium**, which is good for our bones and teeth.

Make a list of foods that contain these nutrients: proteins, carbohydrates, vitamins and minerals, and fats.

## Fats

Foods that contain **fats** help our nervous system.

## Fruits and vegetables

Fruits and vegetables contain lots of **vitamins** and **minerals**. Vitamins keep us healthy and minerals help us grow.

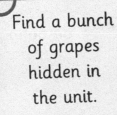

Find a bunch of grapes hidden in the unit.

Which of these snacks is healthy?

# Investigate    STAGE 1

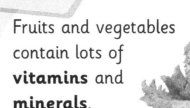

- **You are in charge of the school kitchen for a day! With a partner, make a menu. Remember to make the menu balanced and include foods from all the food groups.**
- **Compare your menu with another pair.**

For breakfast, we have chosen ... because ...

That's interesting. We have chosen ...

¹**balanced:** with the right amount of different things

21

# CAN YOU CHEW WITHOUT YOUR TEETH?

When you eat food, your **digestive system** breaks it down into **nutrients** that your body needs.

**1** The process of digestion begins in the **mouth**. Here, the **teeth** break the food down into smaller pieces.

**2** The **oesophagus** pushes the food down into the **stomach**.

mouth

**3** The **small intestine** separates the nutrients from the waste.

oesophagus

**4** The **nutrients** pass from the small intestine into the **blood**, which carries them to all parts of the body.

stomach

small intestine

**5** The **waste** moves to the **large intestine** and leaves the body through the **anus**.

anus

large intestine

Put a small cracker in your mouth and keep it on your tongue. Try to chew it without using your teeth. What happens? How does digestion begin?

Look at the digestive machine. Can you label its parts?

# HOW FAST DOES YOUR HEART BEAT?

By the end of this lesson, you will know how nutrients and oxygen reach all parts of the body.

The **circulatory system** is made up of the heart and thousands of tubes called arteries and veins.

The heart pumps **blood** around the body.

The blood travels through the **arteries** and **veins**, and carries nutrients and oxygen to all parts of the body.

Measure how many times your heat beats in a minute. Then, jump up and down 20 times. What happens to your heart beat when you exercise?

heart

left atrium

veins

arteries

right venticle

The **heart** is made up of four sections: the left and right **atriums**, and the left and right **ventricles**.

# Investigate  STAGE 2

- Write down the parts of the digestive system and the circulatory system.
- Close your eyes and try to say the organs in order.
- With a partner, write down sentences about how the circulatory system and the digestive system work together.

23

## HOW LONG CAN YOU HOLD YOUR BREATH FOR?

Your **respiratory system** helps you breathe. When you breathe in, you take in the **oxygen** your body needs from the air. When you breathe out, you expel the **carbon dioxide** that your body does not need.

By the end of this lesson, you will understand how the circulatory and respiratory systems help transport oxygen around your body.

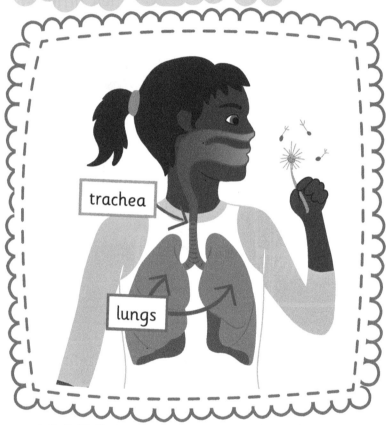

trachea

lungs

1 We breathe in through our **nose** and **mouth**.

2 The air enters the **lungs**.

3 **Oxygen** from the air passes into the **circulatory system** and the blood carries it to all parts of the body.

4 We also breathe out **carbon dioxide** through our nose and mouth.

How long can you hold your breath for? Why can we not do it for a long time?

Under the lungs there is a big muscle called the **diaphragm**, which helps us breathe.

## Look back

Look back to Unit 1. Which part of the brain controls our breathing?

## Investigate    STAGE 3

- Write down the parts of the respiratory system.
- Explain to your partner how the circulatory system and the respiratory system work together.
- Focus on the number of syllables and the stress in each word.

cir-cu-*la*-t(o)ry

re-*spi*-ra-t(o)ry

## BREATHE IN, BREATHE OUT

# Hands on...

### Before you start
Air is a gas. This means that it can move into spaces such as the lungs and fill them.

### Materials
plastic bottle, three balloons, scissors, two straws, elastic bands, plasticine

### Method
1 Cut off the bottom off the plastic bottle.

2 Tie a knot in the neck of a balloon and cut off the fat end.

3 Stretch the balloon over the cut end of the plastic bottle.

4 Insert the straws into the two other balloons. Secure them with the elastic bands.

5 Put the straws with balloons on them into the bottle and seal the neck of the bottle with plasticine.

6 Hold the bottle and pull the knot of the balloon.

### Conclusions
What happened when you pulled the knot of the balloon?

What happened when you released the knot?

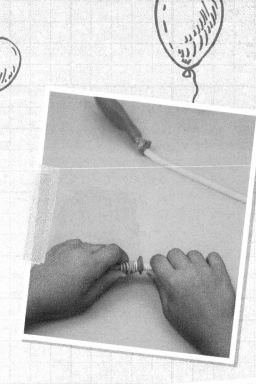

This balloon represents the diaphragm. When we breathe in, does it go up or down?

When I released the knot, the ...

When I pulled the knot, the ...

## WHY DO YOU SWEAT?

The **excretory system** is a group of organs that help eliminate waste from the body.

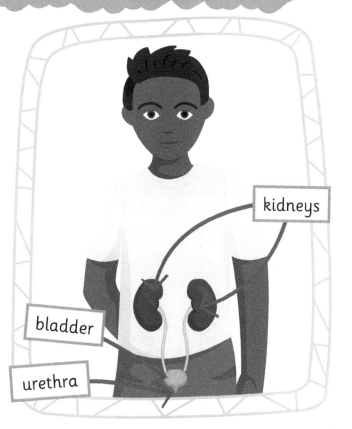

kidneys

bladder

urethra

1 The **kidneys** remove waste from the blood.

2 The waste combines with water to make **urine**.

3 The urine passes to the **bladder**, where it is stored.

4 The urine leaves the body through the **urethra**.

Did you know your body also eliminates waste through the skin? This waste is a liquid called sweat. We sweat when we get hot.

## Investigate   STAGE 4

- With a partner, practise saying the parts of the excretory system in order.
- Choose one of the foods from your menu in Stage 1. With a partner, write down what happens to this food after it enters the body.
- Think about the role that each body system plays.

### Look back

Blood carries some waste to the kidneys. What other substances does the blood carry?

26

## DO YOU GET ENOUGH SLEEP?

U

By the end of this lesson, you will understand how important it is to sleep well.

What are healthy habits? Eating a balanced diet is good for our health but what about exercise and sleep? Do you do some exercise every day? Do you get a good night's sleep? If not, you might be stopping your brain from developing into a super brain!

### Exercise

Experts say exercise is good for our minds, and improves our ability to focus. Try doing some exercise when you are studying for a test and see if it helps you concentrate.

Exercise also makes us happy! As we exercise, hormones are released which improve our mood and self-esteem.

We should do around 60 minutes of aerobic activity a day. Think about all the moments in a day when you are active. Are you reaching your 60 minute goal?

### Sleep

Scientific evidence shows that sleep is as important for our development as eating a healthy diet and having regular exercise.

Experts say sleep helps the brain develop, especially in growing children. Between the ages of 5–11, we need about 10 hours sleep a night.

If we do not sleep well, we do not function well. We find it hard to concentrate, we make more mistakes and we feel grumpy!

How many hours did you sleep last night? How do you feel today?

Log how much sleep and exercise everyone in your class gets during a week. Think about how to reach your sleep and exercise goals!

**1** **Choose the correct word. Test your partner.**

a *How / Which / When* nutrient gives us energy?

b *Why / What / Where* does digestion begin?

c *What / Which / When* do the kidneys remove from the blood?

d *Which / What / How* do the body systems work together?

> Digestion begins in …

**2** **In your notebook, complete the sentences using *which*, *where* or *whose*.**

a The oesophagus is the part of the body ..... pushes food down into the stomach.

b The small intestine is ..... the nutrients are separated from the waste.

c The diaphragm is a big muscle under the lungs ..... helps us breathe.

d The bladder is ..... urine is stored.

**3** **Rewrite the sentences.**
**Change the word in bold into two words.**

a By the end of this unit, **you'll** understand how the circulatory system works.

b The **stomach's** an organ in the digestive system.

c **We're** made up of body systems that work together.

d The heart is a muscular organ. **It's** divided into four parts.

e **We've** got two lungs.

**1** **Read the text and copy it in your notebook. Write the correct word next to letters a–d.**

It is very important to eat food from different food groups because different nutrients help our body in different ways. Calcium is good for our (a) ..... and bones. (b) ..... give us energy. Fruit and (c) ..... give us vitamins and minerals. Proteins and iron make our (d) ..... strong.

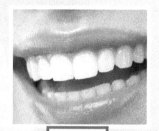

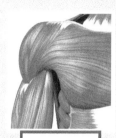

| teeth | muscles | milk | vegetables | carbohydrates |

**Now choose the best name for the text.**

A healthy diet        A day in the supermarket        A big surprise

**2** 🎧 **Listen and choose *a*, *b* or *c*.**

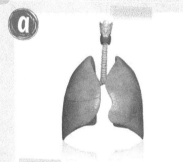

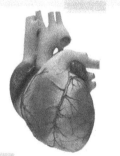

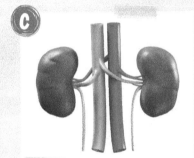

## Investigate   FINALE

- Work with a partner to arrange your description from Stage 4 into a rap.
- Focus on the pronunciation of the key words.
- Think carefully about the rhythm you want to create. Decide how you will accompany the rap – with music, a beat, clapping or something else.
- Perform your rap for the rest of the class.

This is our rap. We hope you like it!

**Assessment link**

Go to page 80 for more activities.

# 3

# WHICH VERTEBRATE HAS *TWO LIVES?*

## Look and see...

Can you name the animals in the photos?
Where do they live?

Which vertebrate groups do these animals belong to?

What invertebrates can you see?

**S ng**
The vertebrate song

**D CUMENTARY**
The animal kingdom

# Investigate

In this unit, you will give a presentation about animals that can be found in the same country. To do this, you will:

- learn the characteristics of vertebrates and invertebrates.
- choose a country and find out about the animals that live there.
- make a fact-file about one mammal, one bird, one reptile, one amphibian, one fish and one invertebrate that live in your chosen country.

# WHAT TYPE OF VERTEBRATE ARE WE?

By the end of this lesson, you will know what we have in common with a lion.

We can classify animals into two groups: **vertebrates** and **invertebrates.** Vertebrates have a **backbone** and invertebrates do not have a backbone. We can also classify vertebrates into **five smaller groups**: mammals, birds, reptiles, amphibians and fish.

## MAMMAL CHARACTERISTICS

### Nutrition

Mammals can be **carnivores**, **herbivores** or **omnivores**. All baby mammals drink their **mother's milk**.

### Respiration

All mammals breathe with their **lungs**.

### Reproduction

Almost all mammals are **viviparous**. Their babies are born live.

Monotremes are mammals that lay eggs. They are oviparous.

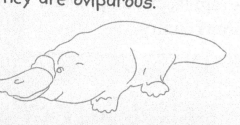

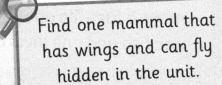

### Physical characteristics

Most mammals live on **land** and have **four legs**.

Some mammals live in **water** and use **flippers** to move.

Most mammals have **fur** or **hair** to keep them warm.

Find one mammal that has wings and can fly hidden in the unit.

# WHY CAN'T YOU FLY?

By the end of this lesson, you will know why most birds can fly ... and why you cannot!

There are many species of **birds**. They can be different colours and sizes, but they all **share some characteristics**.

## BIRD CHARACTERISTICS

### Nutrition

Like mammals, birds can be **carnivores**, **herbivores** or **omnivores**. Adult birds **feed their chicks** when they are young.

### Respiration

Birds breathe with their **lungs**, also like mammals.

### Reproduction

Unlike mammals, birds are **oviparous**. They reproduce by laying eggs. The baby bird develops inside the egg.

### Physical characteristics

Most birds can fly. They have **wings**, a **tail** and **feathers**, which help them fly.
Unlike mammals, birds have **light**, **hollow bones**, which help them fly. A bird's feathers keep it warm. All birds have a **beak** for eating.

Find out which birds cannot fly.

## Investigate · STAGE 1

- Choose a country. Investigate the mammals and birds that live there. Look for interesting information about these animals.
- Make a fact-file about one mammal and one bird.

|  | MAMMAL | BIRD |
| --- | --- | --- |
| Name |  |  |
| Nutrition |  |  |
| Respiration |  |  |

## HOW DO SNAKES MOVE?

By the end of this lesson, you will understand how reptiles can survive in hot climates.

Crocodiles, snakes and turtles look very different from each other, but they belong to the same vertebrate group. They are all **reptiles**.

## REPTILE CHARACTERISTICS

### Nutrition

Almost all reptiles are **carnivores**, but some are omnivores.

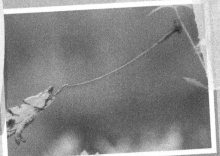

### Respiration

Reptiles, like mammals and birds, breathe with their **lungs**.

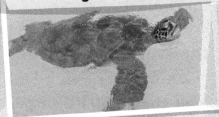

### Reproduction

Most reptiles are **oviparous**.

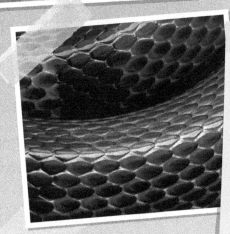

### Physical characteristics

Reptiles have **scales**, which provide them with camouflage and protect them from injury. Scales also prevent water evaporation, which means that reptiles do not need much water to survive.

Most reptiles have **arms** and **legs**, which they use to walk and run. Other reptiles swim. Snakes have no legs, so they slither.

Reptiles live mostly on land, but some spend time in water. Find out where these aquatic reptiles lay their eggs.

## Investigate — STAGE 2

- Investigate some reptiles that live in your chosen country.
- Choose one and make a fact-file about it.
- Practise describing your reptile to a partner. You can add extra bits of interesting information.

This reptile is a carnivore / omnivore / herbivore.

It eats …

# NOW YOU SEE ME, NOW YOU DON'T!

## Hands on...

**Before you start**

Many animals use camouflage to hide from animals that want to eat them. Other animals use camouflage to hide from the animals they want to eat.

**Materials**

a newspaper, different coloured paper, scissors, glue

**Method**

1 Draw outlines of different animals on a single page of newspaper and cut them out.

2 Draw the same animal outlines on coloured paper and cut them out.

3 Stick all of your animal cut-outs on a double page of newspaper.

4 Test your classmates. Can they find all the animals?

**Conclusions**

Which animals is it difficult to see?

Why is it difficult to see them?

Can you *see* the animals hiding in these photos?

It's difficult to see ...

The ... animals are well hidden.

35

## WHAT IS METAMORPHOSIS?

**Amphibians** are very interesting animals. Young amphibians do not look like their parents. They transform as they grow. This transformation is called **metamorphosis**.

## AMPHIBIAN CHARACTERISTICS

**Nutrition**

Most amphibians are **carnivores**.

**Reproduction**

Amphibians are **oviparous**.

**Respiration**

Baby amphibians live in water and breathe through their **gills**, like fish do. Adult amphibians breathe with their **lungs** and through their **moist skin**.

The word *amphibian* means *two lives*: one in the water and one on land.

**Physical characteristics**

Unlike reptiles, amphibians do not have scales. They have **moist skin** which absorbs oxygen.

What must a frog develop before it can live on land?

Frogs are amphibians. Let's look at how they transform ...

1  Frogs **lay eggs** called frogspawn.

**Tadpoles** hatch from the eggs.

3  The tadpoles grow **back legs**.

4  Then, they grow **front legs**.

5  Finally, they **lose their tail** and move on to the land.

# WHY CAN'T YOU BREATHE UNDER WATER?

By the end of this lesson, you will know how fish breathe.

**Fish** live in water. Some fish, such as tuna, live in the sea or ocean (salt water). Other fish, like carp, live in rivers and lakes (fresh water).

## FISH CHARACTERISTICS

Why do we use the term *salt water* to describe the sea and ocean?

### Nutrition

Fish are a mixture of **carnivores**, **herbivores** and **omnivores**.

### Respiration

Fish take in the oxygen they need from water, using their **gills**.

### Reproduction

Almost all fish are **oviparous**. They lay lots of eggs under water.

### Physical characteristics

Fish have **scales**, like reptiles do. The scales act as armour and protect them from injury. Scales also help fish to swim, as do their **fins**.

Find out about a fish that is not oviparous.

## Investigate STAGE 3

- Investigate fish that live in your chosen country.
- Choose one and make a fact-file about it.
- Work with a partner and ask each other questions.

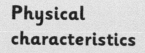

What does your fish eat?

My fish is a ... and eats ...

37

## ARE YOU AFRAID OF SPIDERS?

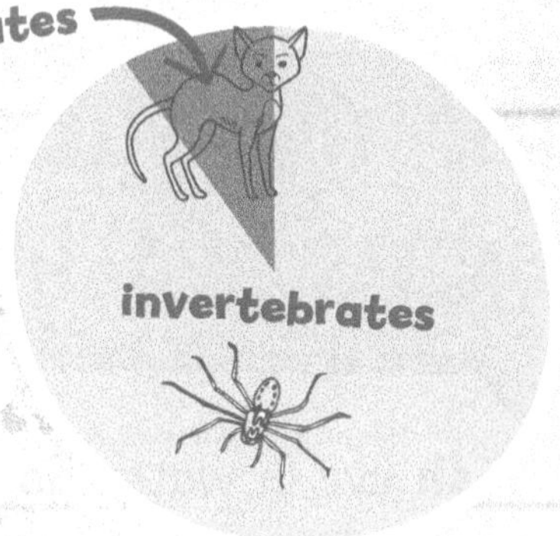

vertebrates

invertebrates

Invertebrates are the **largest group of animals** on Earth. There are many different types of invertebrates. Some live in water and others live on land. They can walk, crawl[1], swim or fly. We classify them into smaller groups, but they all share one characteristic: they **do not have a backbone**.

## ARTHROPODS

Arthropods are the largest invertebrate group. There are **four smaller groups** of arthropods:

### Arachnids
- exoskeleton
- eight legs
- most have eight eyes

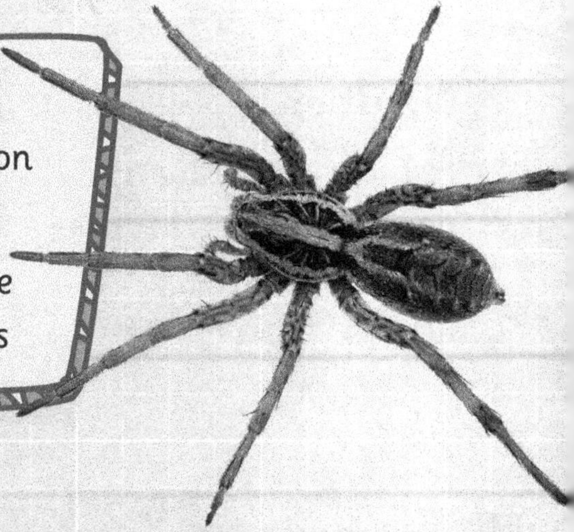

### Insects
- exoskeleton (an external skeleton)
- six legs
- two antennae
- most have wings

Write down three examples for each type of arthropod.

### Myriapods
- exoskeleton
- segmented[2] body
- two antennae
- many legs

### Crustaceans
- hard exoskeleton
- most have eight legs
- most have two claws
- four antennae

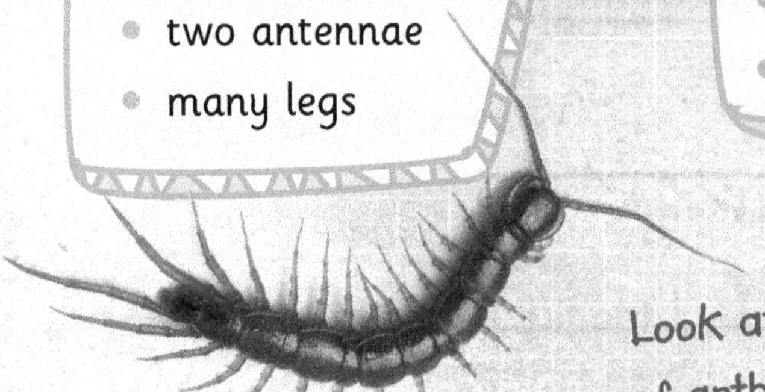

Look at the different groups of arthropods. What do they have in common?

38

# MOLLUSCS

Molluscs are another large group of invertebrates.

By the end of this lesson, you will understand why a spider is not an insect.

## GASTROPODS

They have a **shell** for protection.

**Gastropods** have **soft bodies**.

What do all molluscs have in common?

They do not have a **shell**.

## CEPHALOPODS

They use their **tentacles** to move through the water.

**Cephalopods** also have **soft bodies**.

## BIVALVES

**Bivalves** have two shells that open and close.

They have a soft body.

**Look back**

Which body system allows you to move?

There are other invertebrate groups. Two examples from them are on this page. Find out which invertebrate groups they belong to.

# Investigate — STAGE 4

- Investigate some arthropods and molluscs that live in your chosen country.
- Choose one and make a fact-file about it.
- Ask a partner yes-or-no questions about their chosen invertebrate. Guess what group it belongs to.

Does it have eight legs?

Can it fly?

[1]**to crawl:** to move from one place to another, close to the ground
[2]**segmented:** made up of different sections

**1** 🎧 **Listen and write the answers in your notebook.**

Ella's pet

a  What animal is it?

b  Is it big or small?

c  What colour is it?

d  Where does it live?

e  How old is it?

f  What is its name?

**2** **Compare the two animals using the words in the box.**

faster   stronger   bigger
smaller   slower   more colourful

**3** **Complete the text about birds in your notebook.**

Birds can be of many different sizes and colours. All birds (**a**) ..... oviparous. They (**b**) ..... two wings, feathers and a beak. Most birds (**c**) ..... fly, but some birds, such as penguins and ostriches, (**d**) ..... fly. All birds (**e**) ..... a beak.

**1** **Complete the sentences in your notebook.**

a ..... have a backbone.

b ..... do not have a backbone.

c Carnivores eat other animals. ..... eat plants and ..... eat plants and other animals.

d There are five vertebrate groups: birds, ..... fish, ..... and ..... .

e ..... animals lay eggs, but ..... animals are born live.

f ..... and ..... are two groups of invertebrates.

**2** **Match. Copy the sentences into your notebook.**

a Amphibians     are mostly viviparous and drink their mother's milk.

b Mammals     have scales and breathe through their gills.

c Reptiles     change through a process called metamorphosis.

d Birds     have scales and breathe through their lungs.

e Fish     have a beak, two wings and feathers.

f Arthropods     have exoskeletons.

# Investigate   FINALE

- Find photos of the animals that live in your chosen country.
- Practise talking about the animals in your country using your fact-files and photos.
- Present your country's animals to a partner or the whole class.

> Today, we are going to visit the amazing world of ...

- Remember to speak clearly and look at your audience!

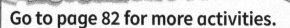

**✓Assessment link**

Go to page 82 for more activities.

# 4

# HOW DO PLANTS GET THEIR FOOD?

## Look and see...

Can you identify the seasons by looking at these trees?

How many of these plants can you name?

Which of these plants does not need a lot of water to survive?

Song
Parts of a plant

DOCUMENTARY
The plant kingdom

# investigate

In this unit, you will investigate the plants in your neighbourhood and make a field journal. To do this, you will:

- take photos or draw pictures of plants in your local area and identify their parts.
- classify these plants as flowering or non-flowering.
- describe the reproduction of flowering plants.
- gather all the information together in your field journal.

# CAN YOU MAKE CELERY TASTE SWEET?

**Plants** are the largest group of living things on Earth. They can grow almost anywhere, for example in hot deserts or in dark forests. Plants can be tall, like trees, or tiny, like mosses. Most plants have **three parts**: roots, a stem and leaves.

**A** The **leaves** are where the plant makes its food, with the help of sunlight.

**B** The **stem** gives the plant support. Water and minerals are transported through the stem to the rest of the plant.

**C** The **roots** hold the plant in the ground. They also absorb the water and minerals that the plant needs.

Do you know what this process is called?

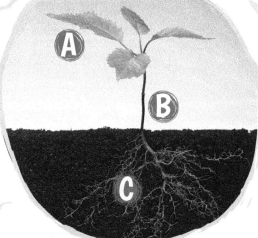

## Try this ...

Check out this easy experiment! Eat a small piece of celery. Do you like its bitter taste? Put a celery stem in a glass of water mixed with sugar. Wait for a few hours and taste the celery again. Explain what has happened.

# HOW DO YOU KNOW HOW OLD A TREE IS?

By the end of this lesson, you will understand the differences between trees, bushes and grass.

We **classify** plants in different ways. One way we classify them is by their **stems**.

**Trees** are the tallest plants. They have high branches and a hard, thick stem called a trunk.

Did you know that you can find out how old a tree is by counting the rings inside its trunk? They have one ring for each year of their life.

Grasses are also known as herbaceous plants.

**Bushes** are shorter than trees. They have low branches. Many bushes have more than one hard stem.

**Grasses** usually have a short, thin stem. The stems are usually flexible and bend in the wind!

## Investigate  STAGE 1

- Find plants in your local area. Take photos of them. You can also draw pictures of them.
- Label the parts of the plants.
- In pairs, classify your plants as trees, bushes or grasses.

This plant is a ...

You can see its ...

# HOW DO PLANTS REPRODUCE?

We can also classify plants by how they reproduce. There are two groups: **flowering plants** and **non-flowering plants**.

## FLOWERING PLANTS

**Angiosperms**

- Produce **flowers** and **fruit**.
- **Seeds** develop inside the fruit.
- Examples include apple trees and roses.

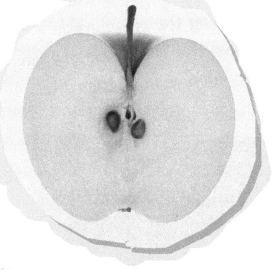

Use the internet to find more examples of angiosperms and gymnosperms.

Focus on the correct pronunciation of *angiosperm* and *gymnosperm*. How many syllables does each word have?

**Gymnosperms**

- Do not produce fruit.
- Seeds develop inside **cones**.
- Most gymnosperms are evergreen trees.

## NON-FLOWERING PLANTS

- Do not reproduce with seeds.
- Reproduce with **spores**.
- Plants release[1] spores into the air.
- Examples include **mosses** and **ferns**.

spores

Did you know that you can grow a plant without using seeds or spores? Cut the top off a carrot and place it on a plate with a little water. Observe what happens.

Spores are very small but very resistant. After a forest fire, ferns and mosses are the first plants to grow again.

 Find the cone hidden in the unit.

**Look back**

Which of the plants on pages 42–43 are non-flowering?

 **STAGE 2**

This is a flowering plant. It is an angiosperm because …

- **Look at the images of your plants from Stage 1.**
- **In groups, classify them as flowering or non-flowering. Include extra interesting information.**
- *If you are not sure how to classify your plants, use the internet to help you.*

[1] **to release:** to allow something to move freely and independently

# WHY ARE PETALS SUCH BEAUTIFUL COLOURS?

By the end of this lesson, you will know the role petals play in the reproduction of flowering plants.

Did you know that the **reproductive organs** of a flowering plant are inside its **flowers**? These reproductive organs make seeds that later grow into new plants.

**Petals** come in lots of different colours, which attract insects.

The **stamens** produce pollen. Insects carry the pollen to other flowers.

The **carpel** is where the seeds grow. It has two parts: the **stigma** and the **ovary**.

**Sepals** are small leaves. They protect the flower before it opens.

When pollen lands on the stigma of a plant, it travels to the ovary. The ovary grows into a fruit. The seeds develop inside the fruit.

**Pollen** is also transported by the wind.

# Investigate   STAGE 3

- Look for an example of an angiosperm in your neighbourhood. Bring a sample into school.
- Dissect and examine it using a magnifying glass.
- Separate the different parts. Use transparent sticky tape to stick the reproductive organs onto small pieces of paper and label them.

## TIME TO WAKE UP!

# Hands on...

### Before you start

Germination is when a seed begins to grow into a plant. A seed will only grow into a plant if the conditions are correct.

### Materials

four small cups, four seeds (beans, lentils, chickpeas, etc.), soil, stickers, water

### Method

1 Put a seed into each cup. Put soil into three of the four cups.

2 Label the cups: *no water*, *no light*, *no soil* and *control*.

3 Place the *no light* cup in a cupboard. Place the other cups in a sunny part of the room.

4 Add a little water to each cup, except the one marked *no water,* every day.

5 Check the results after a week.

### Conclusions

Which beans have germinated?

Which have grown the best?
Did any seeds die?

What do seeds need to germinate?

This experiment shows us that seeds need ...

Archaeologists in Israel found some seeds when they were excavating ancient ruins. They planted the seeds and a few weeks later, a plant began to grow. The plant was a palm tree and the seeds were about 2,000 years old.

# WHAT IS PHOTOSYNTHESIS?

How do plants get the **food** they need to grow?
Animals eat plants and other animals. But what do plants eat?

## Recipe for plant food

**Ingredients**

Light energy from the sun
Water and minerals from the soil
Carbon dioxide from the air

Plants make their own food. This process is called **photosynthesis**.

For photosynthesis to take place, plants need: **water**, **minerals**, **light energy** from the sun, and **carbon dioxide**.

Where do plants get the things they need to make their food? Which parts of a plant help to get these things? Look at the recipe on this page to help you.

Let's look at how photosynthesis works.

1 Water and minerals are absorbed from the soil by the roots.

2 They are then transported through the stem to the leaves.

3 The plant takes in[1] light energy from the sun and carbon dioxide through the leaves.

4 The light energy helps the water, minerals and carbon dioxide react to make the food.

5 The food is then transported to all parts of the plant.

6 Photosynthesis also produces oxygen. The plant releases the oxygen into the air.

Why is the oxygen produced by plants important for the planet?

Photosynthesis is made up of two words. *Photo* means light and *synthesis* means to put together.

# Investigate  STAGE 4

- Bring in an angiosperm from your neighbourhood. Try to include the roots.
- Examine the leaves, stem and roots with a magnifying glass.
- In your notebook, write a paragraph explaining how these parts help the plant make its own food.

[1] **to take in something:** to absorb something

51

**1** Rewrite the questions in your notebook and answer them.

> Is a rose prettier than a cactus? Yes, it is.

a Is a rose **pretty** than a cactus?

b Is a tree **short** than a bush?

c Are grasses **thin** than trees?

d Are trees **tall** than daisies?

e Are grasses **strong** than trees?

**Remember the rules**

short – shorter

big – bigger

pretty – prettier

**2** What is it made of? Look at the photos and write sentences in your notebook.

> It is made of …

**a** 100% COTTON

40° Warm Wash

Do Not Bleach

Warm Iron

Dry Cleanable

**b**

**3** Read the conversation and choose the best answer.

1 **Sarah:** Oh no! My plant is dying!

**Chris:** .....

2 **Sarah:** I don't understand. It's been next to the window and had plenty of light.

**Chris:** .....

3 **Sarah:** Of course. It's had plenty of air too.

**Chris:** .....

4 **Sarah:** I did forget! I'm so silly.

**Chris:** .....

a Did you leave the window open?

b I'll buy you another one! But don't forget to water it.

c That's a pity.

d That's strange. Maybe you forgot to water it.

e Great!

**1** Complete the mind map in your notebook using the words in the box.

seeds    bushes    ferns    gymnosperm    grasses

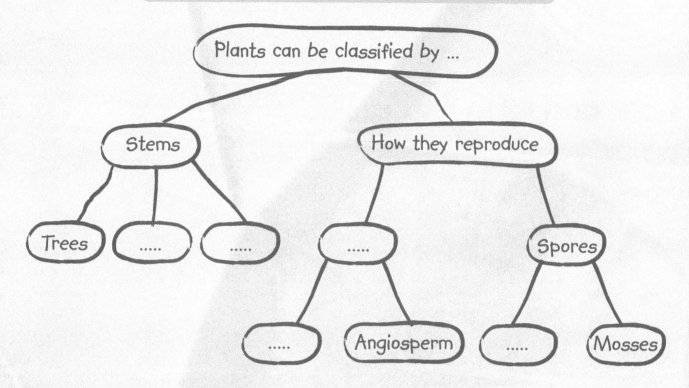

Plants can be classified by ...

Stems

How they reproduce

Trees      .....      .....

.....

Spores

.....      Angiosperm      .....      Mosses

**2** Choose the correct word and write the sentences in your notebook.
a  Plants make food in their *leaves / stems.*
b  *Angiosperms / Gymnosperms* produce seeds inside cones.
c  Ferns reproduce using *spores / seeds.*
d  *Trees / Bushes* have a thick stem called a trunk.
e  Plants produce *carbon dioxide / oxygen* during photosynthesis.

**Investigate**      FINALE

**Assessment link**
Go to page 84 for more activities.

- Organise all your information in your field journal.
- Separate your work into sections: *parts of a plant, classification, nutrition* and *reproduction.*
- Include your photos, drawings, paragraphs and labelled plant parts.
- Exchange journals with a partner, read their information and ask them questions.

## Look and see ...

Can you identify examples of water in its three states: solid, liquid and gas?

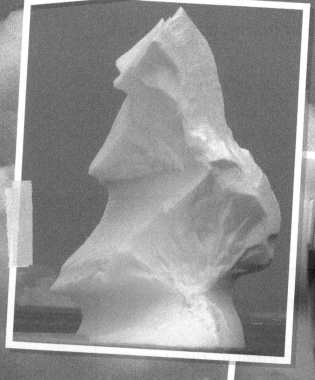

Can you see any examples of mixtures?

What forms of energy can you see in these photos?

**S•ng**
Energy is all around us

**D•CUMENTARY**
Energy and matter

# Investigate

In this unit, you will work in a group to remind people how to save water and energy. To do this, you will:

- investigate ways we use water and the importance of not wasting it.
- learn about how we use electricity in our homes.
- look for ways to save water and energy.
- create signs to encourage your family to save water and energy.

# WHICH STATE ARE YOU IN?

Your pen is made of plastic and your book is made of paper.
But what are plastic and paper made of? They are made of **matter**.
Everything around us is made of matter. Even we are made of matter.

Matter has three **states**. It can be **solid**, **liquid** or **gas**.

### Solid

Solids have a **definite[1] shape**. If you put a ball in a cup, the ball will not change shape. Solids also have a **definite volume**. Volume is the amount of space that matter takes up.

### Liquid

Liquids **do not have a definite shape**. If you pour liquid into a cup, the liquid will change shape to fill the cup. Although liquids change shape, they do have a **definite volume**. In other words, the amount of liquid does not change.

### Gas

Gases **do not have a definite shape** or a **definite volume**. Like liquids, their shape changes to fill[2] the container. Their volume also changes depending on the container they are in.

Water can be found in the three states.

**ice** ↳

**water** ↳

**water vapour** ↳

Find the ice cream hidden in this unit.

Explain how *solids, liquids and gases* are different in terms of *shape and volume.*

## CHANGES OF STATE

Matter can **change state**. Let's look at how water changes from one state to another.

If we heat ice, it melts and changes back into a liquid.
melting

If we heat water, the liquid changes into a gas called water vapour.
evaporation

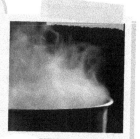

**Ice** **Water** **Water vapour**

freezing
If we freeze water, the liquid changes into a solid called ice.

condensation
If we cool[3] water vapour, it condenses into a liquid.

All living things need water to live. Most of the planet is covered by water, but we can only use a small proportion of it. So we must try to not waste it.

## Investigate — STAGE 1

- Write a list of all the things you do that use water, for example having a shower and washing the dishes.

- Get into groups. Share your information and make a longer group list.

- Use the list to think of ways you can save water at home. Elect one member from the group to write down the ideas.

[3] **to cool:** to make colder
[2] **to fill:** to make a space or container full of something
[1] **definite:** exact, fixed

# WHY DOES ICE CREAM MELT?

**Energy** is everywhere. We cannot always see it, but it is all around us. There are different **forms of energy** and they can change from one form to another.

The sun is the biggest producer[1] of **thermal energy**.

Anything that is hot contains thermal energy. When a substance[2] receives more thermal energy, it might change state.

Can you think of an example of this?

Can you think of other examples of light energy?

The sun also produces **light energy**.

**Look back**

The sun is very important for plants. Can you remember why?

Anything we can hear has **sound energy**. Sound energy travels in waves.

Which forms of energy is electrical energy changed into in the kitchen?

Anything that moves has **kinetic energy**.

Remember the three Rs: reduce, reuse and recycle! Recycling can help save energy. Think about how this is possible.

We use **electrical energy** to make machines work.

Electrical energy can be changed into light, sound, thermal and kinetic energy.

# Investigate    STAGE 2

- Make a list of all the machines in your home that use electrical energy.
- In the same groups as in Stage 1, compare your lists.
- What form of energy does the electrical energy change into? Make a group list.

[2]substance: material
[1]producer: someone or something that makes something

# WHY DO YOU WEAR WOOL IN WINTER?

Materials have different **properties**. Glass is hard and fragile. Plastic is flexible. One of the properties of a material is how **thermal energy** passes through it. Materials can be **insulators** or **conductors** of thermal energy.

By the end of this lesson, you will be able to explain why some materials keep us warm.

## Conductors

Thermal energy passes through conductors quickly. Metals like aluminium are good conductors.

## Insulators

Thermal energy does not pass through insulators quickly. Materials like wool, wood and plastic are good insulators.

Why do we use wooden and plastic spoons when we cook?

Materials can also be electrical conductors or electrical insulators. Electrical wires are made of metal but they are covered in plastic.

## Investigate    STAGE 3

- **Non-renewable energy sources cause pollution. Find out why this happens. Use the internet to help you or ask an expert.**

- **In the same groups, write a questionnaire to find out how people save water and energy at home.**

- **Work with another group and ask them to answer your questionnaire.**

How often do you ... ?

Do you always ... ?

# ENERGY RUSH

## Hands on...

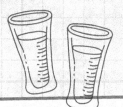

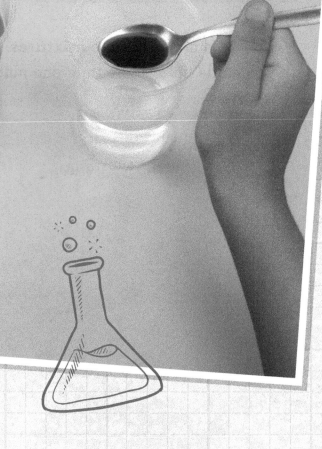

**Before you start**
When a liquid or a gas has more energy, its particles move around more quickly.

**Materials**
cup of hot water, cup of cold water, food colouring

**Method**
1 Put a spoonful of food colouring into each glass.

2 Observe which liquid changes colour more quickly.

**Conclusions**
Which liquid contains more energy: the hot one or the cold one? How do you know?

The ... liquid contains more energy because ...

What happens when we add thermal energy to ice? What happens when we add thermal energy to water? Can you think of more examples?

Thermal energy passes from a warm substance to a cooler substance. The movement of thermal energy is called *heat*. When we touch a hot object, the thermal energy passes from the object to our hand. When we touch a cold object, thermal energy passes from our hand to the object.

# HOW CAN YOU FIND GOLD?

Most things around us are **mixtures**. A mixture is something that is made up of more than one material. There are two types:

1 Mixtures in which **we can see** the different substances.

2 Mixtures in which **we cannot see** the different substances.

**What type of** mixture **can you** see **in each picture?**

I can see different substances in this mixture. There are ...

62

We can **separate** some mixtures, but we cannot separate them all.

By the end of this lesson, you will know how you can separate gold from sand.

We **sieve** mixtures to separate solids of different sizes.

We **filter** mixtures to separate solids from liquids.

We **evaporate** a mixture to separate a solid from the liquid it is dissolved[1] in.

How can we use sieving, filtering and evaporation to separate the mixture of water, pebbles, sand and salt?

Did you know some people wear masks over their mouths? These masks filter pollen, dust, pollution and germs from the air we breathe.

[1] **to dissolve:** to mix a solid with a liquid so that it becomes part of the liquid

63

**1** What *is going to* happen? Copy and complete the sentences in your notebook.

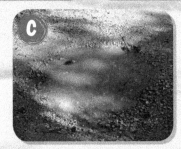

a The water is going to ..... .

b The butter is going to ..... .

c The puddle is ..... .

**2** What *should* we do to help save energy and water? What *shouldn't* we do? Look at the photos and write sentences in your notebook.

**3** Copy and complete the sentences in your notebook.

a If you heat ice, it ..... .

b If you freeze water, it becomes a ..... .

c If you ..... , it changes into water vapour.

d If you cool water vapour, ..... .

**1** Look and read. Choose the correct word for each sentence and write them in your notebook.

sieve      conductors      insulators      solid      energy

a This can be changed from one form to another.
b This state has a definite shape and a definite volume.
c We do this to separate solids of different sizes.
d Thermal energy passes through these easily.
e Thermal energy does not pass through these easily.

**2** Which forms of energy can you see in the pictures? There may be more than one.

# Investigate   FINALE

- Use the results of your questionnaire to think about the best ways to save water and energy.
- Make signs to remind your family or friends to save water and energy.
- Place them around your home or school.

**Assessment link**
Go to page 86 for more activities.

# WHAT IS A SIMPLE MACHINE?

## Look and see...

Which machines have we been using for hundreds of years?

Which machines do you use every day?

**S⬤ng**
Simple machines

Which of these machines need electricity to work?

Which of these machines do we use to communicate?

**D▶CUMENTARY**
Incredible inventions

# Investigate

In this unit, you will design a complex machine. To do this, you will:

- find out about the six simple machines and how they work.
- learn about real life examples of the six simple machines.
- invent your own complex machine made up of simple machines.

# WHICH SIMPLE MACHINE HOLDS THINGS TOGETHER?

We use machines to make work easier. When we think about machines, we usually imagine a **complex machine**, like a computer. However, there is another type of machine – **simple machines**. Simple machines have no moving parts or few moving parts.

## INCLINED PLANE

An **inclined plane** is a surface that goes from a low level to a high level. We use it to move heavy objects up and down.

## SCREW

We use **screws** to hold things together[1] and also to lift objects.

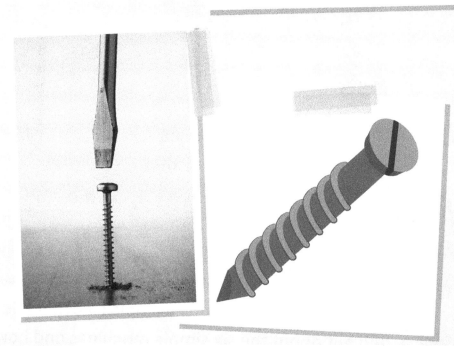

Find a screw hidden in this unit.

When we put simple machines together, we make a **complex machine**.

## MAKE AN INCLINED PLANE

**Materials**
marbles, sandwich bag, elastic band, books, ruler

**Method**

1 Put the marbles in a sandwich bag and seal it. Tie the elastic band around one end of the bag.

2 Put the books in a pile and make a ramp using the ruler.

3 Drag the sandwich bag up the ramp by pulling on the elastic band.

Add more books to the pile. Is it easier or more difficult to pull the marbles up the ramp?

By the end of this lesson, you will know how to move very heavy objects into a lorry.

## MAKE A SCREW

**Materials**
paper, scissors, marker, pencil, sticky tape

**Method**

1 Cut the paper to make a right-angled triangle. Draw a line on the longest side of the triangle.

2 Wrap[2] the paper around the pencil.

3 Stick the paper to the pencil with sticky tape.

## Investigate  STAGE 1

- Find examples of inclined planes in your neighbourhood.
- Make a simple machines table. Add a column for the inclined planes you have found.
- Add another column for examples of screws used in your school.

[1] **to hold (something) together:** to keep two or more things united
[2] **to wrap around:** to put paper or a soft material around an object

69

# CAN YOU MAKE YOUR OWN CAR?

A **pulley** and a **wheel and axle** are two more examples of simple machines.

## PULLEY

We use a **pulley** when we have to lift or lower something heavy. A pulley uses a **wheel** and a **rope** to lift an object.

Many people think that the Ancient Egyptians used inclined planes and pulleys to build the pyramids ... about 5,000 years ago!

## WHEEL AND AXLE

This simple machine is made up of a **wheel** which turns around an **axle**. We use it to move things across the ground more easily, or to apply force more easily.

## MAKE A PULLEY

By the end of this lesson, you will know how to move objects across the ground more easily.

**Materials**
plastic cup, two pieces of string (one long and one short), stones

**Method**

1 Make two holes near the top of the cup and push the short piece of string through them to make a handle[1].

2 Tie[2] one end of the long piece of string to the handle. Pass the other end over a door handle.

3 Put stones in the cup and pull down on the string to lift the cup.

*Is it easier or more difficult to lift the cup with more stones in it?*

## MAKE A WHEEL AND AXLE

**Materials**
cardboard tube, long wooden sticks, four plastic bottle tops

**Method:**

1 Make four holes in the cardboard.

2 Push the wooden sticks through the holes to make two axles.

3 Make a hole in the centre of the four bottle tops and attach them to the axles.

# Investigate    STAGE 2

- **Find four examples of pulleys and wheels and axles that we use in everyday life.**

- **Add them to your table from Stage 1. Circle or colour code the ones that need electricity to work.**

*Does you car move more easily with or without wheels?*

[1] **handle:** the part of an object which you use to carry or open it
[2] **to tie:** to attach one thing to another using string or rope

A **lever** and a **wedge** are two more examples of simple machines.

## LEVER

A lever is made up of a **rigid¹ bar** and a **fulcrum**. When we push one end of the lever down, the opposite end moves up. It is easier to lift an object when we use a lever.

## WEDGE

A wedge is an object with a **slanted² surface**, like an inclined plane. When we push down on the flat part of a wedge, we can cut things easily. We can also use a wedge to stop something moving.

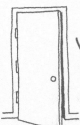

What do you think prehistoric people used wedges for?

**Identify the simple machines on pages 66–67.**

72

## MAKE A LEVER

**Materials**
two pencils, plasticine, a rigid ruler, two plastic cups, marbles, coins

**Method**

1 Stick the pencils to the table with plasticine to make the fulcrum. Place the ruler on top.

2 Stick a plastic cup to each end of the ruler with plasticine.

3 Put marbles into one of the cups. Put coins into the other cup to lift the lever.

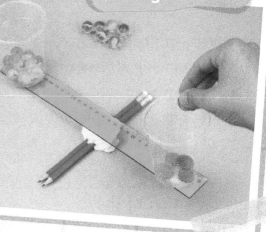

If you move the fulcrum closer to the cup with the marbles, do you need more or fewer coins to lift the marbles?

## MAKE A WEDGE

**Materials**
piece of cardboard, stones, sticky tape

**Method:**

1 Fold the cardboard so that you can see a triangle from the side. Secure it with sticky tape.

2 Put stones inside to make it heavier.

3 Use a door to test the wedge. Does it stop the door from moving?

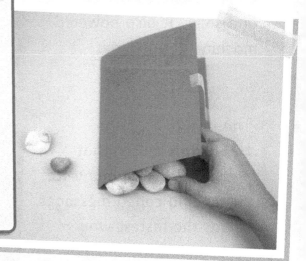

## Investigate    STAGE 3

- Take photos or draw pictures of levers and wedges in your home and at school. Label the different parts of these simple machines.

- Compare what you have found with a classmate. Add them to your table from Stage 1.

There are ... examples of levers in my home.

The ... acts as a lever.

¹**rigid:** not flexible; does not change shape easily
²**slanted:** inclined; sloped in one direction

## WHAT DID WE USE BEFORE SMARTPHONES?

By the end of this lesson, you will understand how inventions change over time.

It is very difficult to imagine a world without machines. **Inventions** usually begin as an idea and are created later. As time passes, people improve and change the inventions to make them better.

The invention of the **steam engine** started the Industrial Revolution. The engine used water vapour, or steam, to do work. The steam engine powered trains and ships. It also powered machines in factories.

Which machine comes between the telegraph and the smartphone?

The invention of the **telegraph** meant that people could communicate by sending coded messages. It was the fastest way of communicating over long distances.

## Investigate     STAGE 4

- With a partner, invent a complex machine that contains different simple machines.
- What does your machine do? Exchange ideas with another pair.

Our machine makes it easier to ...

# Hands On...

**Before you start**

People communicated via telegraph using Morse code – a system of long and short clicks. Morse code can also be communicated using a torch.

**Materials**

torch, pen, paper

**Method**

1 Write your name in Morse code.

2 Work with a partner. Use your torches to communicate your names to each other. Keep the light on for one second to represent a dot (•) and three seconds for a dash (–).

3 Write other words to communicate to your partner. Send them via Morse code. Keep the light on for seven seconds to represent a space between words.

**Conclusions**

Were you able to understand your partner's messages? Were they able to understand yours?

Is it easy to communicate via Morse code?

Compare this method with the machines we use to communicate today.

It is faster / easier to communicate with ... than with ...

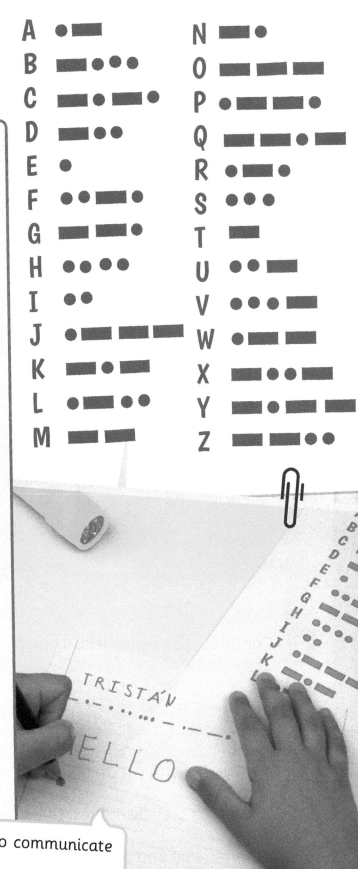

**1** 🎧 **Listen and write the correct letter in your notebook.**

1 Which machine is Jack talking about?

2 Which machine is Emma talking about?

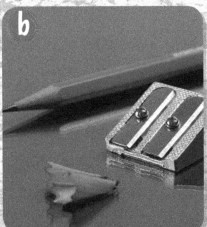

**2** **Complete the sentences using the words in the box.**

into   down   across   around   up

a A wheel and axle helps us move things ..... the floor.

b A wedge can cut an object ..... smaller parts.

c When a bicycle moves, the wheels turn ..... .

d When one end of a lever goes ..... , the other end goes ..... .

**1** How are these simple machines making work easier? Identify the differences in the two pictures.

A

In Picture A they are ... , whereas in Picture B ...

B

This is our invention. It's called the ...

# Investigate FINALE

- With your partner, draw a diagram of your invention from Stage 4.
- Label the simple machines that it contains.
- Present your invention to another pair.

**✓ Assessment link**
Go to page 88 for more activities.

# Questions

## Think about it

1 What is the control centre of the nervous system?

2 Name the five sense organs.

3 Which words are missing from the list? *Hearing, touch, smell, ..... and .....*

4 What carries information from our sense organs to the brain?

5 What vibrates in the ear during the process of hearing?

6 Which sense organ are the iris, pupil and retina part of?

7 What are the two holes in the nose called?

8 Write down six adjectives that describe how things feel.

9 Which word is missing? *Bones, joints and ..... make up the locomotor system.*

10 Which is the odd one out: *elbow, knee, skull* or *hip*? Why?

## Think harder

1 What is the difference between the cerebrum and the cerebellum? Why is the brain stem important?

2 The sense organs perceive different things. Describe what each sense organ perceives. *Our eyes can .....*

3 With a partner, discuss how our senses can keep us out of danger.

4 Describe how information is sent to and from the brain.

5 How can we look after our hearing?

6 Draw a diagram that shows how the eye works.

7 What are the four tastes we can identify? Give an example of each one.

8 With a partner, think about ways that the sense of touch can help people who cannot see.

9 Find out how broken bones heal.

10 Find out how many bones a baby has. Then, find out how many bones an adult has.

# Study aid

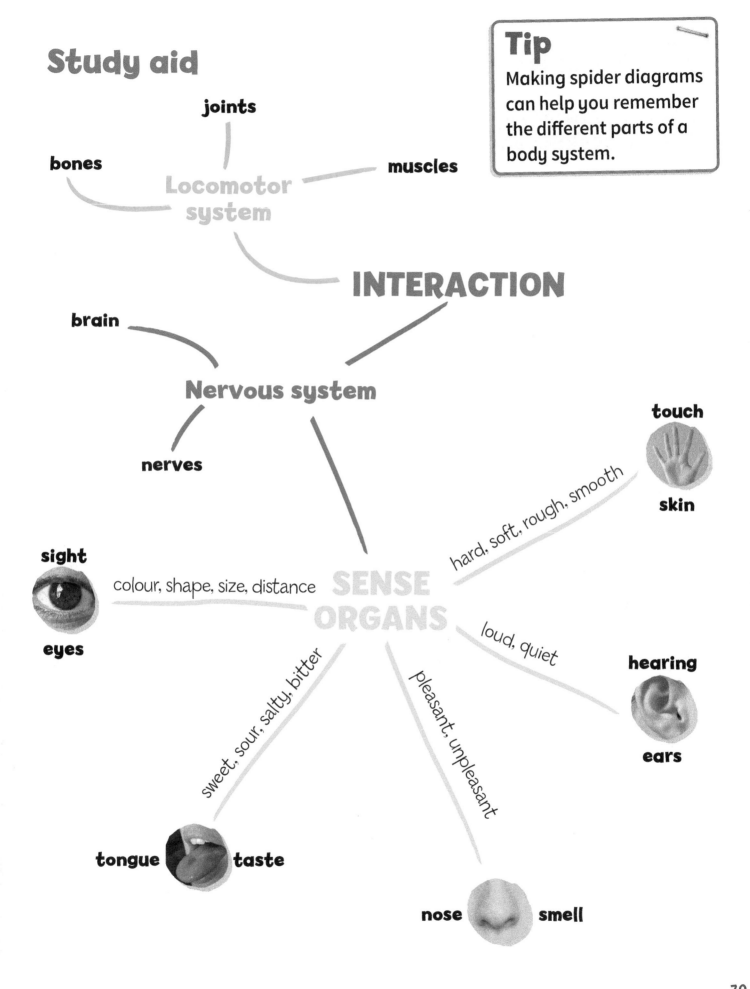

joints

bones

**Locomotor system**

muscles

**Tip**

Making spider diagrams can help you remember the different parts of a body system.

## INTERACTION

brain

**Nervous system**

nerves

touch

skin

sight

*hard, soft, rough, smooth*

*colour, shape, size, distance*  **SENSE ORGANS**

eyes

*loud, quiet*

hearing

ears

*sweet, sour, salty, bitter*

*pleasant, unpleasant*

tongue   taste

nose   smell

## Questions

Think about it

1 Is this sentence true or false?
*Chicken is rich in calcium.*

2 Name the missing nutrient:
*protein and iron, fats, vitamins and minerals, calcium and .....*

3 Tell your partner what you had for breakfast today. Decide if it was healthy or unhealthy.

4 Which body system breaks food down and extracts nutrients from it?

5 When do we sweat?

6 Is this sentence true or false?
*The respiratory system expels oxygen from the body.*

7 In what part of the body do nutrients pass into the blood?

8 Which tube does urine leave the body through?

9 What are the tubes in the circulatory system called?

10 Make a list of healthy habits.

Think harder

1 Explain to a partner why we need to eat food from all the food groups.

2 Explain why our body needs nutrients, e.g. *Carbohydrates give us energy.*

3 Keep a food journal for a week. Did you follow a balanced diet?

4 Make a table which includes the different parts of the digestive system and definitions of what each part does.

5 Find out which tubes carry blood away from the heart and which carry it back.

6 Breathe in and breathe out slowly. Describe what happens to your chest.

7 Explain how the circulatory system and respiratory system work together.

8 Which organs do we excrete liquid waste through?

9 Discuss with a partner why it is important to drink a lot of water. Explain two ways we lose water from our body.

10 Investigate how much sleep a newborn baby needs compared to an adult. Brainstorm why babies need more sleep than adults.

# Study aid

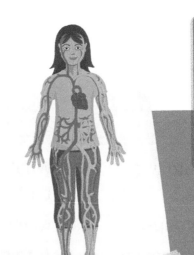

## Tip
Using different colours can help you remember different groups of things ... like body systems!

## CIRCULATORY SYSTEM
heart
arteries
veins

## DIGESTIVE SYSTEM
mouth
oesophagus
stomach
small intestine
large intestine
anus

## RESPIRATORY SYSTEM
nose and mouth
trachea
lungs
diaphragm

## EXCRETORY SYSTEM
kidneys
bladder
urethra
skin

# (3) Questions

## Think about it

1 Animals can be classified into two main groups. What are they?

2 Name the five vertebrate groups.

3 Which of these animals does not lay eggs? *Turtle, lion, frog, penguin.*

4 Do reptiles lay their eggs on land or in water?

5 Which group of vertebrates have feathers and a beak?

6 What is the name of the transformation that amphibians experience?

7 Name three main body parts of a fish.

8 Is this sentence true or false? *Most of the animals on Earth are vertebrates.*

9 Which physical characteristic do all arthropods have?

10 Which invertebrate group do snails and octopuses belong to?

## Think harder

1 What is the principal difference between the two main animal groups?

2 Which characteristics do we look at when we are classifying vertebrates?

3 Explain to your partner the difference between viviparous and oviparous animals.

4 Find out why sea turtles are classified as reptiles when they spend most of their lives in the ocean.

5 Which physical characteristics help birds fly?

6 Describe the process of metamorphosis to your partner.

7 Fish lay thousands of eggs. Find out why.

8 Name a vertebrate and an invertebrate that do not have any legs. How do they move from one place to another?

9 Which invertebrate group do spiders and scorpions belong to? Which characteristics do they share?

10 Discuss with a partner the differences between the three main groups of molluscs.

# Study aid

## Tip

Read – Cover – Write – Check. Some of the names of animal groups are difficult to spell. Copy their names onto a piece of paper. Read the words carefully. Cover the words and write the names. Check your spellings.

### Mammals

Dog

Horse

Whale

### Birds

Duck

Chicken

Ostrich

### Reptiles

Lizard

Crocodile

Turtle

### Amphibians

Frog

Toad

Salamander

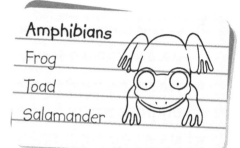

### Fish

Shark

Carp

Trout

### Crustaceans

Lobster

Crab

Shrimp

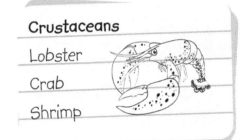

### Insects

Bee

Ant

Butterfly

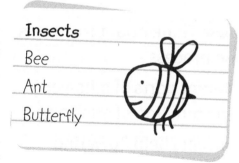

### Arachnids

Scorpion

Spider

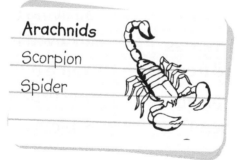

### Myriapods

Centipede

Millipede

### Gastropods

Slug

Snail

### Cephalopods

Octopus

Squid

### Bivalves

Clam

Oyster

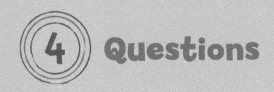

# 4 Questions

1 Name the three parts that most plants have.

2 When we classify plants by their stem, we divide them into three groups. Name them.

3 Is this sentence true or false? *Grasses usually have a short, thick stem.*

4 Where do seeds develop in an angiosperm?

5 Name two non-flowering plants.

6 Name the process by which plants make their own food.

7 Which gas do plants release when they perform photosynthesis?

8 Which part of a flowering plant contains the reproductive organs?

9 What attracts insects to a flowering plant?

10 What do seeds need in order to germinate?

## Think harder

1 Explain the functions of the three main parts of a plant to a partner.

2 What are the different ways that we can classify plants?

3 Explain to a partner the differences between grasses, bushes and trees.

4 What is the difference between an angiosperm and a gymnosperm?

5 How do non-flowering plants reproduce?

6 Explain the process of photosynthesis to a partner.

7 Why is photosynthesis important for all living things? Think about the gases involved in the process.

8 Name the different parts of a flower and explain the function of each one.

9 Explain how insects help flowering plants reproduce.

10 What would happen if there were no plants? How would this affect other living things?

# Study aid

## Classification by stems

trees | bushes | grasses

**Tip**

Representing information in a visual way can help us to remember things more easily. For example, it can help us to remember the different ways of classifying plants.

## Classification by reproduction

**flowering plants**

angiosperms      gymnosperms

fruit      cones

seeds

**non-flowering plants**

mosses      ferns

spores

# (5) Questions

## Think about it

1 What are the three states of matter?

2 Which is the odd one out: *water*, *milk* or *chocolate*? Explain why.

3 What do we call water in its three different states?

4 What happens when we transfer a liquid from one container to a container of a different shape?

5 Which types of energy come from the sun?

6 Give three examples of kinetic energy.

7 Is this sentence true or false? *We wear woollen gloves in winter because wool is a conductor.*

8 Can you name three machines that use electrical energy?

9 Which separation method do we use to separate soil from water?

10 Name two ways of saving water at home.

## Think harder

1 Both solids and liquids have a definite volume. Explain how their shape is different.

2 Describe how we can change water from a solid to a gas.

3 Why does ice cream melt quickly on a hot day? Think about what ice cream is made of.

4 If we leave a cup of water in the sun, the liquid disappears. Why does this happen?

5 Why is the sun so important for plants?

6 A fire engine is going to an emergency. Identify three forms of energy as the fire engine passes by you.

7 Write a definition of the word *heat*.

8 Choose three machines that use electrical energy. What types of energy do they transform electrical energy into?

9 How can you separate a mixture of water, salt and rice?

10 With a partner, talk about why it is important to save energy.

# Study aid

**Tip**

Putting information into tables can help you remember it. You can also draw pictures.

| States of matter | Definite shape | Definite volume |
|---|---|---|
| Gas | X | X |
| Liquid | X | ✓ |
| Solid | ✓ | ✓ |

| Start point | Process | End point |
|---|---|---|
| Gas → | Condensation → | Liquid |
| Liquid → | Evaporation → | Gas |
| Solid → | Melting → | Liquid |
| Liquid → | Freezing → | Solid |

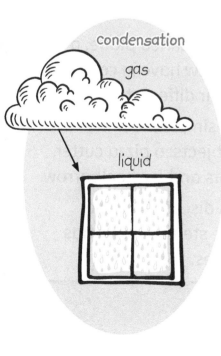

condensation

gas

liquid

evaporation

gas

liquid

freezing

liquid

solid

melting

solid          liquid

# Questions

1 Complete the sentence. *We use machines to make work .....*

2 Is this sentence true or false? *Simple machines have a lot of moving parts.*

3 What do we use inclined planes for?

4 Which simple machine do we use to hold things together?

5 What are the two parts of a lever called?

6 Give three examples of machines that use wheels and axles.

7 Which simple machine can you use to cut a sandwich?

8 How many simple machines use a wheel? What are they?

9 What did people use the telegraph for?

10 Name the odd one out: *smartphone*, *bicycle* and *computer*.

**Think harder**

1 What is the difference between a simple machine and a complex machine?

2 What are the six simple machines? Invent an acrostic to help you remember them.

3 If an inclined plane is steeper, does it make the work easier or more difficult?

4 Identify the different simple machines in a pencil sharpener.

5 What happens when you go on a seesaw with a person that is heavier than you? Think about ways to solve this problem.

6 Use objects from your pencil case to demonstrate how levers work.

7 Talk to your partner about the different simple machines you can use to move a heavy object.

8 Explain what an inclined plane, a wedge and a screw have in common. Think about their different parts.

9 Find out which simple machines are part of these objects: a pizza cutter, a pair of scissors and a wheelbarrow.

10 With a partner, discuss how the invention of the steam engine has changed our lives.

# Study aid

Inclined plane

**Tip**
Using real-life examples can help you remember technical information.

Screw

Pulley

Wheel and axle

Lever

Wedge

89

# 1 More hands on...

**Before you start**
Are you more coordinated with one eye or with two?

**Materials**
small paper cup, five 5 cents coin

**Method**
1 Put the cup in front of your partner. It should be 60 cm from him or her.

2 Ask your partner to close or cover one eye.

3 Hold one of the coins in the air about 50 cm above the table and move it slowly from side to side.

4 Tell your partner to say *Drop it!* when they think the coin is above the cup.

5 Repeat the experiment with both eyes open.

6 Now change places.

**Conclusions**
Were you more successful with one eye or with two eyes?

Were the results the same for you and your partner?

How important are our senses for coordination?
How does sense impairment effect coordination?

# 2 More hands on...

## Before you start

Why are potatoes in the same group as bread and cereals if they are vegetables? Let's find out with iodine – a chemical that turns starch, a type of carbohydrate, blue.

## Materials

plate, apple, carrot, bread, potato, biscuit, rice, cereal, iodine

## Method

1 Place the items of food you are going to test on a plate.

2 Put three or four drops of iodine onto each item of food.

3 Look carefully at the colour of the iodine on the food.

## Conclusions

What colour is the iodine on the carrot?

What colour is the iodine on the rice?

What colour is the iodine on the potato?

What is the main nutrient in potatoes?

### Before you start
What do butterflies eat? Make a feeder to attract butterflies and find out.

### Materials
plastic cup, string, cotton wool, coloured tissue paper, glue, water, sugar

### Method
1 Make two holes in opposite sides of the plastic cup, near the top. Tie some string through the holes to make a handle.

2 Make a hole in the bottom of the cup. Push a pencil through it to make it bigger.

3 Push a small ball of cotton wool through the hole. Half of the ball should be inside the cup and half outside.

4 Cut out petal shapes from the tissue paper. Glue them to the cup, around the cotton ball, to make a flower.

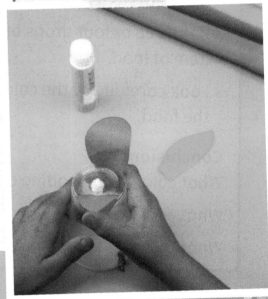

5 Put nine tablespoons of water into a bowl. Add one tablespoon of sugar and stir the mixture. Pour the mixture into the cup.

6 Hang the feeder in your garden, on your balcony or from a window.

### Conclusions
What attracted the butterflies?

What is nectar? How does it taste?

### Before you start
Is an avocado a fruit or a vegetable? The next time your family uses avocado in a salad, ask if you can keep the seed and try this experiment.

### Materials
avocado seed, four toothpicks, small cup, water

### Method
1 Clean the avocado seed carefully.

2 Push the toothpicks into the sides of the seed. The toothpicks stop the seed from falling into the water.

3 Fill the cup with water and use the sticks to balance the seed at the top of the cup. Make sure that the bottom of the seed is touching the water.

4 Change the water after a few days if it looks dirty. Add more water if the seed is not touching it.

### Conclusions
What happened to the avocado seed?

Many people think that tomatoes are vegetables, but they are fruit. Can you explain why? Are foods with seeds *fruits* or *vegetables*?

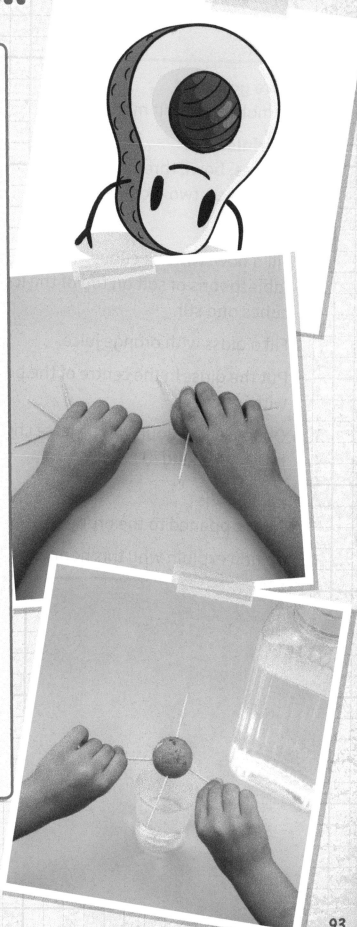

# 5 More hands on...

**Before you start**
Salt makes ice melt more quickly.

**Materials**
ice cubes, bowl, three tablespoons of salt, orange juice, two glasses

**Method**

1 Fill a bowl with ice cubes. Sprinkle three tablespoons of salt on top of the ice cubes and stir.

2 Fill a glass with orange juice.

3 Put the glass in the centre of the bowl with ice cubes.

4 Observe how your orange juice changes before drinking it!

**Conclusions**
What happened to the orange juice?

Can you explain why this happened?

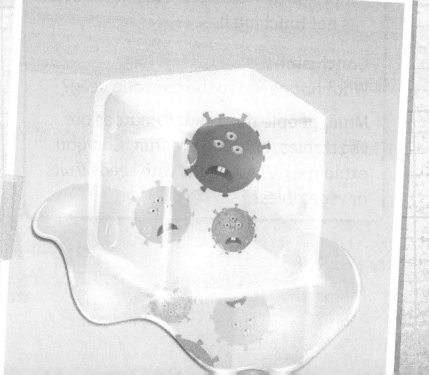

## 6 More hands on...

**Before you start**

During the Middle Ages, catapults were used to attack enemy castles. You can make a small version of a catapult using lollipop sticks and elastic bands.

**Materials**

eight lollipop sticks, four elastic bands, plastic spoon, paper to make balls for the catapult

**Method**

1 Join six lollipop sticks together using two elastic bands. Twist the bands around both ends of the sticks. Make sure that the bands are very tight.

2 Join the other two sticks together with an elastic band at one end only.

3 Push the group of six sticks between the two joined sticks.

4 Twist the final elastic band around the end of the top stick.

5 Push the spoon under the elastic band on the top stick to attach it to the catapult.

6 The catapult is ready to fire. Make some small balls of paper and put them on the spoon.

7 Hold the front of the catapult and push down on the top stick and the spoon.

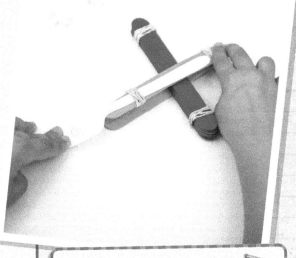

**Conclusions**

Which simple machine are you using when you fire the catapult?

Can you think of ways to make your catapult stronger and better?

**WARNING:** Be very careful when you use the catapult. Be careful not to hit anyone or anything with the paper balls.

**CAMBRIDGE**
UNIVERSITY PRESS

## Acknowledgements

The authors and publishers acknowledge the following sources of copyright material and are grateful for the permissions granted. While every effort has been made, it has not always been possible to identify the sources of all the material used, or to trace all copyright holders. If any omissions are brought to our notice, we will be happy to include the appropriate acknowledgements on reprinting and in the next update to the digital edition, as applicable.

All the photographs are sourced from Getty Images.

pp. 2–3, p. 30: Juan Carlos Vindas/Moment, pp. 2–3, pp. 6–7: cosmin4000/iStock/Getty Images Plus; p.3, p.4, p. 5: Ronnie Kaufman/Larry Hirshowitz/Blend Images; p. 4: Robert Deutschman/Stone, SerrNovik/iStock/Getty Images Plus; pp.4–5: Spaces Images/Blend Images; p. 5: Laurence Monneret/DigitalVision, Ljupco/iStock/Getty Images Plus; p. 5, p. 8: Natasha_Pankina/iStock/Getty Images Plus; p. 6: Hero Images, Zing Images/Photodisc, Steve Satushek/Photodisc, mandygodbehear/iStock/Getty Images Plus, lemonadeserenade/iStock/Getty Images Plus, godfather744431/iStock/Getty Images Plus, Olly-Molly/iStock/Getty Images Plus; p. 6, p. 18, p. 67, p. 72: Westend61; p. 7: angelhell/E+; p. 7, p. 20, p. 21, p. 36: Dorling Kindersley; p. 7, pp. 8–9: SCIEPRO/Science Photo Library; p. 8: Kontrec/iStock/Images Plus, Adie Bush/Cultura; p. 9: Ian Cuming/Ikon Images; p. 9, p. 57: David Harrigan/Canopy; p. 9, p. 15, p. 57, p. 58, p. 70: FrankRamspott/DigitalVision Vectors; p. 9: rvika/iStock/Getty Images Plus; p. 10: Zero Creatives/Cultura; p. 10, p.26, p. 31, p. 45, p. 63, p. 64, p. 83: ourlifelooklikeballoon/iStock/Getty Images Plus; p. 12: Philippe Gelot/Photographer's Choice, sv_sunny/iStock/Getty Images Plus; p. 13, p. 25, p. 35, p. 49, p. 61, p. 75: novaaleksandra/iStock/Getty Images Plus; p. 15: Renate Frost/EyeEm, Kazunori Nagashima/Stone, Georg Szabo/STOCK4B, AnikaSalsera/iStock/Images Plus, MINORU KIDA/amana images, unalozmen/iStock/Getty Images Plus; p. 15, p. 68, p. 72: jamtoons/DigitalVision Vectors; pp. 16–17: Science Photo Library - MEHAU KULYK/Brand X Pictures; p.16: Bubert/iStock/Getty Images Plus; p. 17, p. 79: Armi Fello/EyeEm, p. 17: RusN/iStock/Getty Images Plus, Epoxydude/fStop, Brad Wilson/The Image Bank; pp. 18–19: Caiaimage/Paul Bradbury/CaiaimageA; p. 18: Peter Dazeley/Photographer's Choice, SilviaJansen/E+; p. 18, p. 87: zhemchuzhina/iStock/Getty Images Plus; p. 19: Dissoid/iStock/Getty Images Plus, tacojim/iStock/Getty Images Plus, Bartosz Luczak/iStock/Getty Images Plus; p. 20: Michael Zwahlen/EyeEm, PicturePartners/iStock/Images Plus, Coprid/iStock/Images Plus, Roger Dixon/Dorling Kindersley, AlexRaths/iStock/Images Plus, MoMorad/iStock/Images Plus, Science Photo Library; p. 20, p. 62: Ian O'Leary/Dorling Kindersley; p. 21: Paul Poplis/Photolibrary, Michael Reinhard/Corbis Documentary, Steven Morris Photography, Burazin/Photographer's Choice, Iswan Nawi/EyeEm, atoss/iStock/Images Plus, clintscholz/E+, LUHUANFENG/iStock/Images Plus, Digital Camera Magazine/Future, chictype/iStock/Getty Images Plus, kimberrywood/DigitalVision Vectors, Richard Coombs/EyeEm, TS Photography/Photographer's Choice, Cube/Ikon Images, jerryhat/E+, Helen_Field/iStock/Getty Images Plus; p. 23: Leonello Calvetti/Stocktrek Images/Stocktrek Images, veselinaalexandrova/RooM; p. 25: Teploleta/iStock/Getty Images Plus; p. 26: Hoxton/Ryan Lees/Hoxton; p. 27: Alistair Berg/DigitalVision, Thanasis Zovoilis/Moment; p. 28: Tetra Images, puruan/iStock/Getty Images Plus, pp. 28–29: Julie Anne Images/Moment; p. 29: altrendo images/Altrendo, SHUBHANGI GANESHRAO KENE/cience Photo Library, Savany/iStock/Getty Images Plus, anilakkus/iStock/Getty Images Plus, Philip Wilkins/Photolibrary, PIXOLOGICSTUDIO/Science Photo Library, cosmin4000/iStock, Oleksiy Maksymenko/imageBROKER; p. 30: Javier Fernández Sánchez/Moment, Jim Cumming/Moment, John Macgregor/Photolibrary, Sandro Vannini, Hal Beral/Corbis Documentary, MONTICO Lionel/Hemis.fr; pp. 30–31: Arterra/Universal Images Group; p. 31: Tim Jackson/Oxford Scientific, Babs Boelens/EyeEm, Shumba138/iStock/Getty Images Plus, Gerhard Hofmann/EyeEm, Danita Delimont/Gallo Images, Reinhard Dirscherl/Corbis Documentary, Dhruv Reddy/EyeEm, Frederic Labaune/Moment, perysty/iStock/Getty Images Plus, John Cancalosi/Photolibrary; p. 32: DenBoma/iStock/Getty Images Plus, Dave Fleetham/Perspectives, ULTRA.F/DigitalVision, John E Marriott/All Canada Photos; p. 32, p. 38: S-S-S/iStock/Getty Images Plus; p. 33, p. 40: Don Johnston/All Canada Photos; p. 33, p. 67, p. 74: JTB Photo/Universal Images Group; p. 33: Andreas Schimak/EyeEm, Maarigard/Dorling Kindersley; p. 34: Mint Images - Frans Lanting/Mint Images, Enrique R Aguirre Aves/Oxford Scientific, Leighla Murphy/EyeEm, Jeffrey Coolidge/DigitalVision, Sergey_Peykarov/iStock/Getty Images Plus; p. 35: nikpal/iStock/Getty Images Plus, Matthias Graben/imageBROKER, Jared Hobbs/All Canada Photos; p. 36: Jasius/Moment, F Millington/The Image Bank, C. Allan Morgan/Photolibrary, DEA/S. MONTANARI/De Agostini, Spanishalex/iStock/Getty Images Plus; p. 37: by wildestanimal/Moment, Jeff Rotman/Nature Picture Library, FLPA/Colin Marshall/Corbis Documentary, Devi Sankar/EyeEm; p. 38: Mathisa_s/iStock/Getty Images Plus, Goldfinch4ever/iStock/Getty Images Plus, Alain Caste/StockFood Creative, AlasdairJames/E+, Insh1na/iStock/Getty Images Plus; p. 39: AGF/Universal Images Group, Topic Images Inc./Topic Images, StockFood, VeraPetruk/iStock/Getty Images Plus, Magnilion/DigitalVision Vectors; p. 40,

p. 59: Gallo Images - Martin Harvey/Riser; pp. 40–41: Martin Ruegner/Radius Images; p. 41: mocoo/iStock/Getty Images Plus; p. 42: Rosemary Calvert/Corbis Documentary, Dave Reede/All Canada Photos, Flowerphotos/Universal Images Group; pp.42–43: Mehmet Özhan Araboga/EyeEm; p. 43: igorr1/iStock/Getty Images Plus, Mark Winwood/Dorling Kindersley, Scott Goldsmith/Aurora, Bryan Mullennix, kate_sun/iStock/Getty Images Plus; p. 44: ThomasVogel/E+, Martin Leigh/Oxford Scientific; p. 45: Heinz Wohner/LOOK-foto/LOOK, Thomas Winz/Lonely Planet Images, Photographer Chris Archinet/Moment; p. 45, p. 72: LokFung/DigitalVision Vectors; p. 46: Claire Higgins/Photolibrary, Sian Irvine/Dorling Kindersley; cat_arch_angel/iStock/Getty Images Plus, kiyanochka/iStock/Getty Images Plus; p. 46, p. 85: Doug Steakley/Lonely Planet Images, Scott Smith/Corbis Documentary; p.47, p. 85: Ed Reschke/Photolibrary; p. 47: i_panki/iStock/Getty Images Plus; p. 48: Elvina Kiiamova/iStock/Getty Images Plus; p.49: Roderick Chen/All Canada Photos, Burak Karademir/Moment; p. 50: soleg/iStock/Getty Images Plus, Yuji Sakai/DigitalVision, Sudowoodo/iStock/Getty Images Plus; p. 50, p. 62: Dave King/Dorling Kindersley; p. 51: Matt Gibson/Moment; p. 52: kf4851iStock/Getty Images Plus, Oli4eben/iStock/Getty Images Plus, happyfoto/E+, sassy1902/E+, yuoak/DigitalVision Vectors; pp. 52–53: Michael Duva/Stone; p. 54, p. 87: wenchiawang/iStock/Getty Images Plus; pp. 54–55: Terry Vine/The Image Bank; p. 54: Feng Wei Photography/Moment, Eastcott Momatiuk/DigitalVision, Brigitte Sporrer/StockFood Creative, kcslagle/iStock/Getty Images Plus; p. 55: Laszlo Selly/Photolibrary, Glow Images, Inc/Glow, enviromantic/iStock/Getty Images Plus, Caiaimage/Chris Ryan/Caiaimage, AnnaFrajtova/iStock/Getty Images Plus; p. 55, p. 79: Tetra Images; p. 56: Emely/Cultura, Fuse/Corbis, Glow Cuisine/Glow, Tatiana Maramygina/FOAP, JPM/Image Source, Nopparatz/iStock/Getty Images Plus, jameher/Moment, nikkytok/iStock/Getty Images Plus; p. 57: David Arky, Atomic Imagery/DigitalVision; p. 58: Science Photo Library - SCIEPRO/Brand X Pictures, Frozenmost/iStock/Getty Images Plus, seanscott/RooM; p. 59: Bloomberg, Hoxton/Tom Merton, Booblgum/iStock/Getty Images Plus; p. 60: aluxum/iStock/Getty Images Plus, Ariel Skelley/DigitalVision, artisteer/iStock/Getty Images Plus; p. 61: All kind of things in photo/Moment, Xu Wan Y/EyeEm, lhfgraphics/iStock/Getty Images Plus, sunnysideeggs/iStock/Getty Images Plus; p. 62: Martina Gruber/EyeEm, ClaudioVentrella/iStock/Getty Images Plus, kivoart/E+, Mint Images/Mint Images RF, Nadore/iStock/Getty Images Plus, Suzifoo/E+, Robert Kneschke/EyeEm, kizilkayaphotos/E+, molotovcoketail/DigitalVision Vectors; p. 63: Matt Meadows/Photolibrary, Studio Blond, AlbertoLoyo/iStock/Getty Images Plus; p. 64: Taranbir Sawhney/EyeEm, Gregory_DUBUS/iStock/Getty Images Plus, David Crespo/Moment, WP Simon/Photodisc, Charlie Dean/Caiaimage, Fancy/Veer/Corbis/Corbis; pp. 64–65: Vitoria Holdings LLC/iStock/Getty Images Plus; p. 65: JazzIRT/iStock/Getty Images Plus, KidStock/Blend Images/Getty Images Plus, Modoc Stories/Aurora, Chris Winter/Cultura; pp. 66–67: prchaec/iStock/Getty Images Plus; p. 66: Tomekbudujedomek/Moment, Tim Bird/Moment, Dave and Les Jacobs/Blend Images, Education Images/Universal Images Group; p. 67: Julianali/iStock/Getty Images Plus, Maskot, Matthew Shaw/Moment; p. 68: BCFC/iStock/Getty Images Plus, Martin Poole/DigitalVision; p. 70: EnricCoromina/iStock/Getty Images Plus, Keng88Photography/iStock/Getty Images Plus, mushroomstore/iStock/Getty Images Plus; p. 72: Gabriele Ritz/EyeEm; p. 74: Fox Photos/Hulton Archive, Violetastock/iStock/Getty Images Plus, Tim Robberts/The Image Bank, DNY59/iStock/Getty Images Plus; p. 76: Jeffrey Penalosa/EyeEm, Matias Castello/EyeEm, Roy Gumpel/The Image Bank, Tim Graham/Getty Images News, fotoARION - Specialist in product and business photography/Moment, PATSTOCK/Moment, azzzya/iStock/Getty Images Plus, pp.76–77: Anton Eine/EyeEm; p. 79: melking/iStock/Getty Images Plus, Science Photo Library/Getty Images Plus; p. 83: mightyisland/DigitalVision Vectors, ElenaLux/iStock/Getty Images Plus, AllAGRI/iStock/Getty Images Plus, mhatzapa/iStock/getty Images Plus, lineartestpilot/iStock/Getty Images Plus, colematt/iStock/Getty Images Plus, ValentAin_Jevee/iStock/Getty Images Plus, GreenTana/iStock/Getty Images Plus, SKETCHIT/iStock/Getty Images Plus; p. 87: Qilli/iStock/Getty Images Plus, Rkaulitzki/iStock/Getty Images Plus, MilanaAdams/iStock/Getty Images Plus, AntheiaLeia/iStock/Getty Images Plus; p. 89: SolStock/E+, Will Heap/Dorling Kindersley, Hakan Jansson/Maskot, Resolution Productions/Blend Images, Johner Images, Phaitoon Sutunyawatchai/EyeEm; p. 90: Frankie_Lee/DigitalVision Vectors; p. 91: IgorZakowski/iStock/Getty Images Plus; p. 92: Hafizal Talib/EyeEm; p. 94: Sergey Balakhnichev/iStock; p. 95: Sami Sarkis/Photodisc.

Front cover photography by Dave King/Dorling Kindersley/Getty Images, brainmaster/E+/Getty Images, tunart/E+/Getty Images, Pobytov/E+/Getty Images, Brian Macdonald/DigitalVision/Getty Images, Martin Ruegner/Radius Images/Getty Images, Niall Benvie/Nature Picture Library/Getty Images, Mike Hill/Photographer's Choice/Getty Images, Ioannis Tsotras/Moment/Getty Images, leisa hoppe/FOAP/Getty Images, Steve Bloom/The Image Bank/Getty Images.

**The authors and publishers would like to thank the following illustrators:**
Sara Lynn Cramb (Astound US) pp 10, 11 (c), 12 (c), 14 (brain), 15 (l), 17, 22, 23 (heart), 24, 26 (c), 27, 68 (cr, br), 70 (tc, bc), (tc, c), 81; Alejandro Milà (Sylvie Poggio Artists Agency) pp 16 (t), 40, 77 (A, B).